0.7   Cort   S ott
367
bout
L eng

—

what about the Wankel Engine?

what
about
the
Wankel Engine?

110077

by SCOTT CORBETT

illustrated by JEROME KÜHL

FOUR WINDS PRESS
NEW YORK

Library of Congress Cataloging in Publication Data

Corbett, Scott.
    What about the Wankel engine?

    SUMMARY: A general discussion of engines and their his-
tory with emphasis on the Wankel rotary engine and its
many advantages.
    1. Wankel engine—Juvenile literature. 2. Gas and oil
engines—Juvenile literature. [1. Wankel engine. 2. En-
gines] I. Kühl, Jerome, illus. II. Title.
TL210.7.C67   629.2′504   74–8593
ISBN 0–590–07369–9

Published by Four Winds Press
A Division of Scholastic Magazines, Inc., New York, N.Y.
Text copyright © 1974 by Scott Corbett
Illustrations copyright © 1974 by Scholastic Magazines, Inc.
All rights reserved
Printed in the United States of America
Library of Congress Catalog Card Number: 74–8593
2   3   4   5   78   77   76   75

contents

1
will
the wankel
win?

Engines play an important part in the lives of every one of us. Directly or indirectly, we depend on them for heat, light, power, and transportation, as well as for many other things.

An engine is a machine that can turn energy into mechanical force and motion. The source of energy may come from something that can be burned, from chemicals, from nuclear power, from air, or from water.

For the better part of a century one engine has been king of the motorcar world. You would find it under the hood of most cars that have ever been built. It is called the reciprocating piston engine.

Other engines have been used in cars, but in the past none has been able to challenge this one. To do so, a new engine would have to be at least some of the following things:

Cheaper to build.
Cheaper to run.
Smaller and lighter with the same power.

More dependable and long-lasting.

Easier to repair.

Quieter and more nearly vibration-free.

Today several new kinds of engines are being developed, any one of which may eventually perform better than the piston engine. But the one many experts feel shows the greatest promise is the Wankel rotary engine.

The Wankel engine is cheaper to build. Eventually it may cost only half as much as a piston engine of similar horsepower.

It is not yet cheaper to run, but future improvements may make it so. Even now it has the advantage of working well on cheaper, low octane gasoline, and it gives good mileage in city driving—much better than the engines used in large cars.

A Wankel is smaller and lighter than a piston engine of similar horsepower. It weighs less than half as much, and takes up only a quarter as much space under the hood.

Tests indicate that it may well prove to be more dependable and long-lasting, and it is much easier to repair. It has only half as many parts as a piston engine, and less than half as many working parts.

Because its rotor revolves, instead of pounding up and down like pistons, the Wankel is much quieter and more nearly vibration-free.

Later on, when we have learned how the Wankel rotary engine works, we will come back to these points and talk about them in detail. But to understand the Wankel engine and how it works, it helps to learn something first about earlier engines and how man began making engines in the first place.

2

early engines

Man spent a long time on earth, perhaps a couple of million years, before he invented anything more than a few hand tools and weapons. His first great invention was the wheel.

The wheel seems an obvious thing to us now, of course, because we see wheels everywhere and always have. They have always been part of our world. But try to imagine a world in which they were unknown.

If there was no such thing around, how would anyone happen to think of it? To invent the wheel was a remarkable achievement, because nothing that is truly like a wheel exists in nature.

Until the wheel was invented, there could be no engines.

And even after it had been invented, many more thousands of years passed before man produced anything that could be called an engine.

To begin with, there was the question of power. In order to operate, an engine must have a source of power. What an engine actually does is harness raw power of some sort so that it can be put to work.

The first sources of power man used were water and air.

Water power ran the first real engine.

It was invented in Egypt only two thousand years ago, and engines like it are still in use. A chain of buckets strung around two wheels was used to raise water from a stream.

Its source of power was a small waterfall or cascade. Instead of filling buckets from the stream and carrying them up the bank, men raised the water by means of this simple engine.

Each bucket was filled and pushed along by the waterfall. When the bucket reached a point near the top wheel, it was tipped so that the water in it emptied into a trough. *(Figure 1)*

Water was also used to operate water wheels. These were turned by the current of a stream flowing alongside a mill. The power produced by a water wheel was used to turn a millstone, which ground grain to make flour.

Such engines worked well as long as the water supply stayed the same. If the stream dried up, however, the engine stopped working. If heavy rains made the stream rise, its current became too powerful and sometimes destroyed the water buckets or the water wheel.

Twelve more centuries passed before the next important

Figure 1

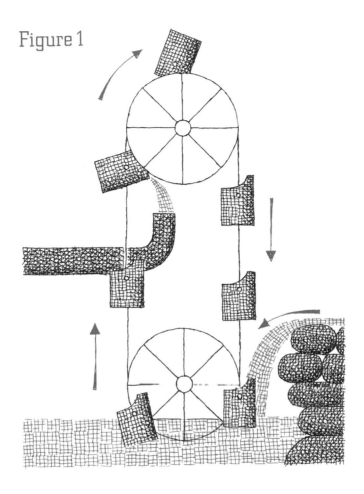

engine was developed. This time the source of power was air.

The engine was the windmill.

During the next seven hundred years windmills were used principally to grind grain. Since then they have been used, and are still used in many places, to pump water or to generate electricity.

A windmill's sails turn a shaft horizontally. But a millstone must rest on another stone so that it can grind the grain between them, and therefore, its shaft must be vertical. So the power produced by the wind that pushed the windmill's sails around had to be made to "turn corners."

This was accomplished by the wheel with another important invention added to it: gears.

By putting teeth or pegs on the rim of a wheel, man invented gears, which can make power "turn corners."

A peg-wheel mounted on the end of the horizontal shaft was fitted into a second peg-wheel mounted on a vertical shaft, and the vertical shaft passed along the power that turned the millstones. *(Figure 2)*

But windmills work only when the wind is blowing hard enough to turn their sails. What man needed was a source of power that could keep engines going whenever he wanted them to work.

Even before windmills or water wheels were developed there were men who knew what this source of power should be. Soon after the bucket chain had been invented, men were already beginning to understand that the answer was fire.

It was a long time, however, before anyone could put fire to work effectively in an engine.

As early as A.D. 50 a Greek named Hero (who also lived in Egypt, in Alexandria) thought up the first steam engine. It was only a toy engine, though, and could not be used for any practical work.

Hero's engine was a hollow ball mounted on hollow pipes. The ball could spin freely on them, and steam could be blown inside it through one of the pipes.

Fitted to the ball on opposite sides were two short, crooked

Figure 2

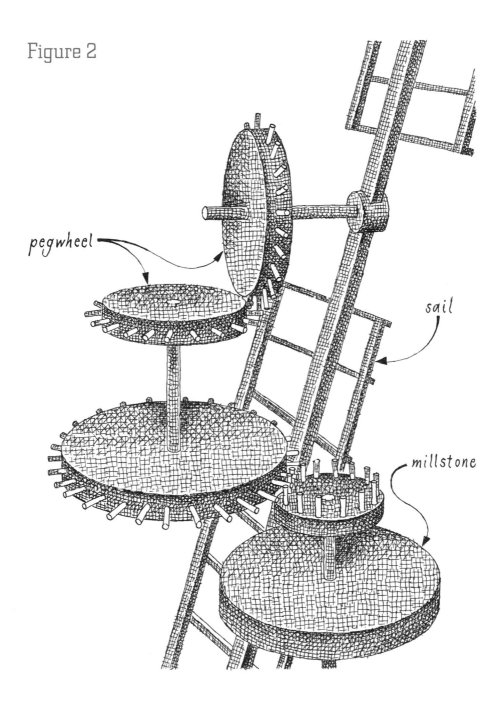

pegwheel

sail

millstone

Figure 3

nozzles through which the steam could escape. The escaping jets of steam set the ball spinning. (*Figure 3*)

Not enough power could be produced in this way, however, to do any useful work. Another sixteen centuries passed before men began to learn how to make steam engines produce real power.

And when the first practical steam engines were finally developed, the power was not produced by the steam itself, but by air.

3

steam engines

The source of power in this new engine was not wind, but air pressure, or atmospheric pressure, as it is usually called.

The earth is surrounded by a layer of air hundreds of miles high, and even though it is light and invisible, air has real weight.

Imagine a column of air one inch square extending up from the earth as far as air reaches. That column of air would weigh about 15 pounds.

For this reason, air exerts a pressure on any surface it touches of 15 pounds per square inch. A 15-pound weight is pressing against every square inch of our bodies right now. The reason this great pressure does not collapse our bodies and kill us is that we have air inside us as well as outside, pressing equally in all directions.

sides of the piston, first underneath it, then above it.

This made the piston work in both directions, so that the rocking beam was no longer needed to pull the piston rod up after each downward power stroke.

Now the steam engine produced two power strokes where it had formerly produced only one. And thus it could do twice as much work.

As far as engines were concerned, the eighteenth century and the first half of the nineteenth were the Age of Steam.

The first vehicles that moved on a level surface without being pushed or pulled by men or animals or propelled by sails were moved by steam engines.

As early as 1770 a Frenchman named Joseph Cugnot had built a three-wheeled "horseless carriage," powered by a steam engine, which could lumber along at three miles an hour for short distances through the streets of Paris. *(Figure 5)*

Unfortunately it overturned on its second trip and scared people half to death. The records are sketchy as to what happened after that, but the story is that Cugnot was thrown in jail and forbidden to build any more of these devilish carriages.

Other men continued to tinker with steam engines, however, and nearly sixty years later, in England, a man with the wonderful name of Goldsworthy Gurney had not only built three steam coaches but had put them into operation on a route near London that covered over three thousand miles.

Again, however, the world was not ready to put up with such contraptions. Within a few years laws were passed in England which made it almost impossible to operate steam coaches on the roads. One of these laws required that a man had to walk

Figure 5

ahead of the coach carrying a red flag by day and a red lantern by night. Furthermore, steam engines were charged heavy tolls on toll roads and bridges.

The result was that the development of "horseless carriages" was delayed for another sixty years or so, until 1896, when the motorcar forced the repeal of the restrictive laws.

In the meantime, however, the steam engine had come into its own as a train locomotive, pulling strings of cars on tracks. The world might not be ready for horseless carriages, but it welcomed the iron horse.

By this time, of course, steam engines had become much more powerful.

The boilers of the engines James Watt was building were in the form of square boxes. A box is a very poor container for steam. The hotter steam becomes, the greater its pressure becomes. Watt's boilers could not take much pressure, because a box has too many seams, which soon begin to leak.

But before long, better boilers were developed, cylindrical in form, and it became possible to build up greater pressures.

In Watt's day, steam pressure could only be developed to about 14 pounds per square inch—less than atmospheric pressure. By the time he retired in 1800, other men were building boilers that could deliver pressures of 60 pounds per square inch.

But steam engines were wasteful. Only a small part of the wood or coal they consumed was transformed into power.

The reason was that the steam had to be heated outside the engine and then be blown into it. In the course of this transfer from the boiler to the engine a lot of heat was lost and wasted.

What was needed was an engine that could burn some sort of fuel *inside* itself, so that less heat would be lost.

As far back as 1678 a Dutch physicist was thinking along the right lines.

However, his choice of a possible fuel was alarming. He suggested explosive charges of gunpowder. And like all the early experimenters he thought only of atmospheric pressure as the source of the power stroke.

Later on, coal gas, turpentine, and naphtha were tried as

fuels, with coal gas proving the most satisfactory. But the right fuel to make engines work really well—something widely available and not too expensive—was still lacking.

Then, in 1859, the first oil well was drilled at Titusville, Pennsylvania. Petroleum became available. But it took several years more before anyone realized that one of petroleum's by-products, which at first no one thought was of any value, might be the answer. (A by-product is something that is produced in addition to the principal product, which in this case was petroleum.) This by-product was called gasoline.

The Dutchman had been right about one thing. Explosive combustion was the answer. A fuel was needed which would explode forcefully and burn up quickly. And gasoline mixed with air was the fuel to do the job.

Gasoline made a success of the engine we have been using ever since, the internal combustion engine.

4
the otto

"Internal combustion" means "burning inside." An internal combustion engine burns fuel inside itself. A great deal of heat is produced in the form of rapid, controlled explosions. Every effort is made to keep all this heat inside the engine and make it work to produce power.

There are several kinds of internal combustion engines, including diesels and rotaries, but the one used in most cars is the four-stroke reciprocating piston engine, sometimes called the Otto.

The man who built the first successful internal combustion engine a hundred years ago and gave his name to all such engines was a German, Nikolaus August Otto. His engine, using benzine for fuel, "worked so elegantly and so beautifully that it would have given an angel joy to watch it," he later declared.

How does it work? Well, it won't work at all without fuel, so let's start by examining that.

Gasoline will burn readily, but when it is mixed with air the mixture becomes explosive. A spark will make it blow up.

The mixture will blow up even more quickly and powerfully if it is first compressed.

To produce the necessary explosion, three things must be done:

First, mix gasoline and air together into a mist.

Second, put this mixture in some sort of chamber where it can be pressed into a smaller and smaller space.

Third, strike a spark into it to make it explode.

The mixing is done in a device called a carburetor.(*Figure 6*)

As air rushes through a passage in a carburetor, a few drops of gasoline are sprayed into it from a nozzle. The spray must be very fine, so that tiny droplets of gasoline spread evenly through the air.

From the carburetor the fuel mixture passes into the intake manifold. This is a chamber above the cylinders.

The place where the explosion and burning of the fuel mixture will take place, however, is in the cylinders.

The fuel mixture flows into the cylinder when the intake valve in the top of it opens. Remember the valves used in steam engines? These valves work much the same way.

Figure 6

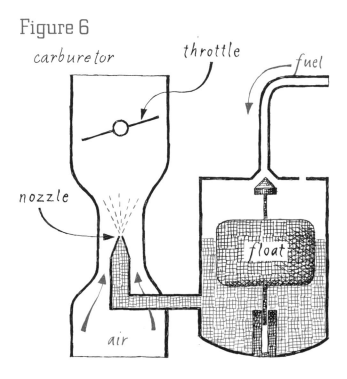

carburetor   throttle   fuel

nozzle

float

air

They are controlled by a special kind of lopsided wheel called a cam.

A cam is like a wheel with a bump on it. The end of the piston's stem touches the cam. When the cam turns and the bump comes under the stem, it pushes up the stem, which lifts the valve. As soon as the bump moves on, the stem slides down and the valve closes again. (*Figure* 7)

The intake valve is timed to open just as the piston has finished its upward movement inside the cylinder and is sliding down again.

As it slid up, the piston drove nearly all the air out of the combustion chamber in the top of the cylinder.

As it slides down, the piston leaves more and more empty

WHAT ABOUT THE WANKEL ENGINE?

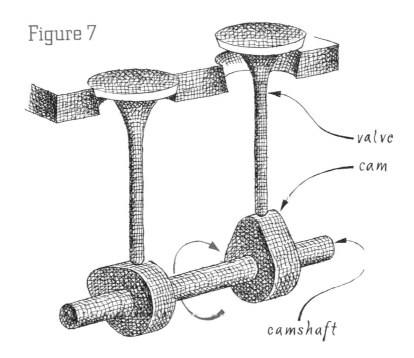

Figure 7

valve

cam

camshaft

space above it. The amount of air left in the combustion chamber is thinned out as it tries to fill the extra space, so that air pressure inside the cylinder drops. A partial vacuum is formed. When the intake valve opens, the fuel is sucked into the vacuum.

It rushes into the cylinder and fills the chamber above the piston. The intake valve closes, trapping the fuel inside. And by now the piston has reached the bottom end of its stroke and is sliding up again inside the cylinder. It pushes hard against the mixture of air and gas, jamming it into a smaller and smaller space.

This action is called compression.

Have you ever been jammed into a subway train or a

Figure 8

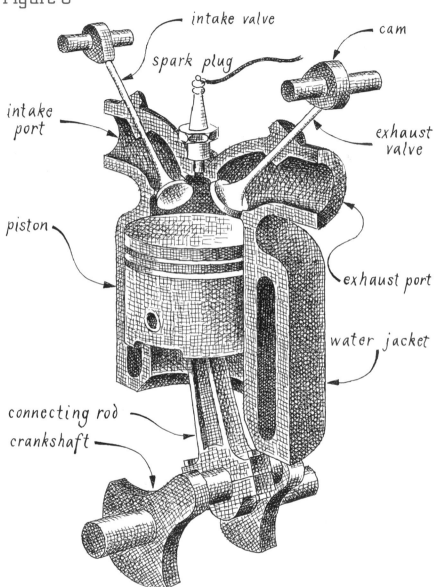

intake valve

cam

spark plug

intake
port

exhaust
valve

piston

exhaust port

water jacket

connecting rod

crankshaft

bus with a lot of other people? Jammed in so closely you could hardly breathe? If you have, you must have found that you were not only uncomfortable but that you became a lot warmer.

Something like this happens when molecules of air are jammed together. Have you noticed how hot a bicycle pump grows when you pump up a tire? When you pump air into a tire you are doing work, which produces heat, and that heat has to go somewhere. The compressed air becomes hotter.

The smaller the space the fuel mixture is jammed into by the piston, the hotter it becomes. The hotter it becomes, the more ready the fuel is to explode.

Now the spark plug goes to work.

The spark plug sticks down into the cylinder chamber. It is connected to the car's battery. When the piston slides up to the top of its stroke, having pressed the fuel into as small a space as it can, a spark jumps between the points of the spark plug. This makes the fuel explode and burn.

The force of the explosion pushes the piston down again. This is the power stroke, the stroke that does work.

Pushed to the bottom of its stroke, the piston starts sliding up again. The fuel has been burned up. All that is left of it is exhaust gases.

Now the exhaust valve opens, so that as the piston rises it can push the exhaust gases out of the chamber.

Once it has pushed out the exhaust gases, the piston starts down again. The exhaust valve closes. The intake valve opens again. A new supply of fuel is sucked in by the piston, and the four-stroke process begins all over again: 1. Intake. 2. Compression. 3. Combustion. 4. Exhaust.

THE OTTO

Figure 9

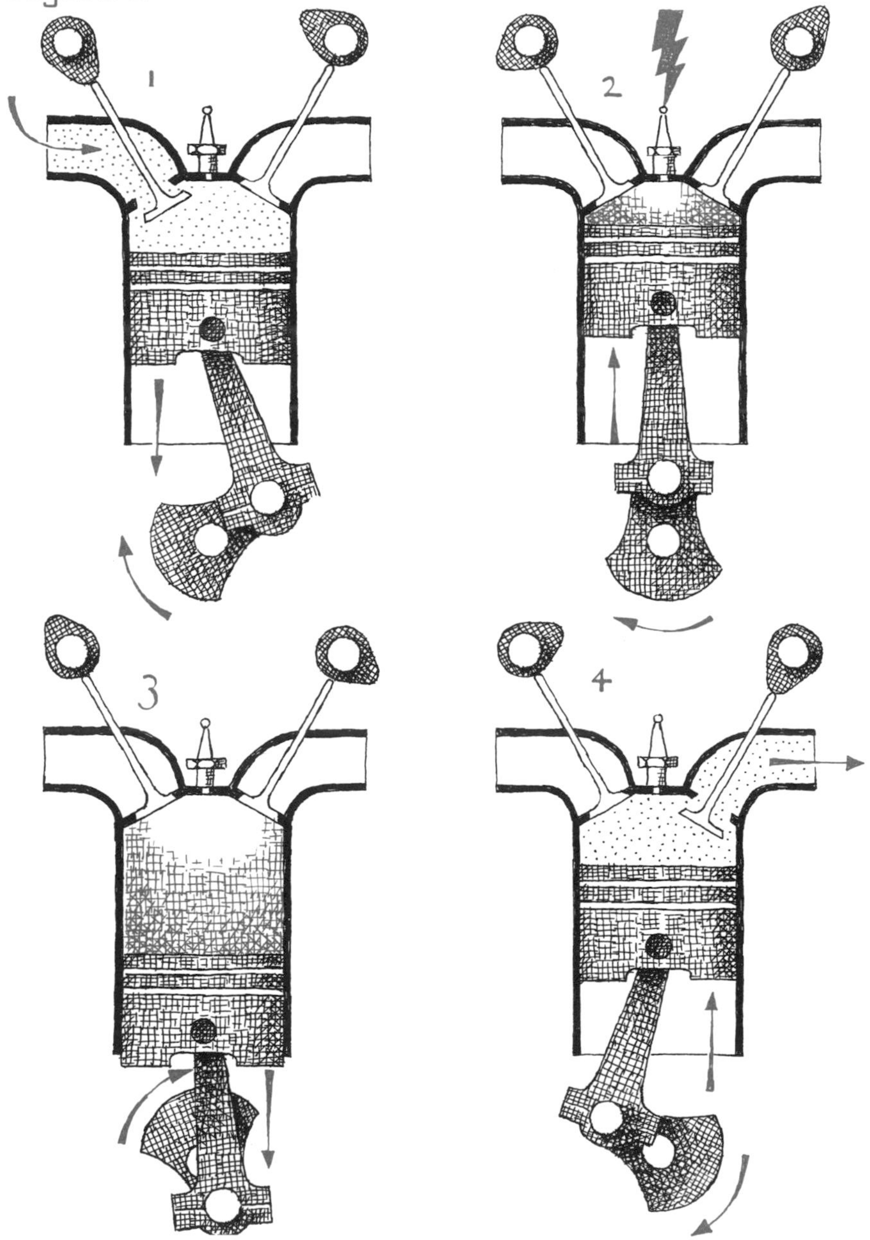

Why is this called a "reciprocating piston" engine?

"Reciprocating" means a to-and-fro motion, or back-and-forth, or up-and-down—a motion that involves reversing direction. In this case, the pistons constantly move up and down, up and down, and pass along their power to the crankshaft.

Each piston is attached by a connecting rod to a V-shaped crank which it swings around, making the crankshaft revolve. The crankshaft carries this power to the axles, which turn the wheels of the car and make it move. Sometimes the power goes to the rear wheels, sometimes to the front ones (front-wheel drive), and sometimes to both sets (four-wheel drive).

As in the windmill, gears are used to make power turn corners—much more efficient gears than were used in the early windmills!

Notice that the piston went up and down twice during the cycle of intake, compression, combustion, and exhaust: two strokes up and two strokes down. This is why it is called a "four-stroke" cycle. Each time a piston goes up and down it turns the crankshaft one full turn. So the crankshaft makes two revolutions during each four-stroke cycle. (*Figure 9*)

But there is only one power stroke during that time.

This means that if a car had to depend on only one cylinder it would be coasting three-quarters of the time, carried along by its own movement, or momentum.

Supposing you were in a swing, with a friend pushing you, but he only gave you a push every other time you swung back to him. You would continue to swing, but you would not swing quite so high the times he did not give you a push as when he did.

If a car had only one cylinder, then its piston rod would turn the crankshaft only once in every two revolutions the crank-shaft made, and even during that one time it would turn it only halfway around. This on-and-off power would not make for a very smooth and steady ride.

Car engines have at least four cylinders, however, and many have six or eight. The cycle of each of these cylinders is timed differently, so that each delivers its power stroke at a different instant.

In this way the crankshaft is receiving a power stroke from at least one cylinder during each half-revolution, instead of only one power stroke per two revolutions. This makes cars run smoothly and steadily.

5

two-strokes
and
diesels

With the piston going up and down twice, each cylinder in the Otto engine is doing a lot of work to produce a single power stroke. Can the same work be accomplished somehow by a two-stroke cycle?

It can. There are also two-stroke reciprocating piston engines that accomplish intake, compression, combustion, and exhaust all in the course of one trip up and down by the piston.

Since the four operations take place during only two strokes, they must be combined in some way, and must happen much more quickly than in the four-stroke cycle.

The two-stroke engines do not have any valves. Instead they have ports, which are simply round holes.

One is the intake port, the other the exhaust port. They are

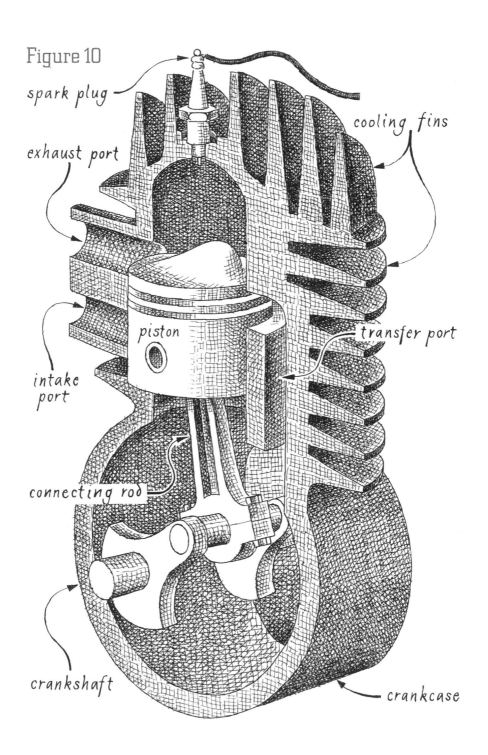

Figure 10

spark plug

exhaust port

cooling fins

piston

transfer port

intake port

connecting rod

crankshaft

crankcase

covered and uncovered by the piston as it slides up and down.

Here the fuel mixture is first sucked into the crankshaft beneath the piston rather than into the chamber above it. The fuel comes in when the piston slides up and uncovers the intake port. But the combustion chamber is still in the same place, above the piston.

When the piston slides down, it uncovers the exhaust port and covers the intake port. As it comes down the piston forces the fuel mixture in the crankcase to flow through a side channel up into the combustion chamber.

Now the piston rises again, compressing the fuel mixture. The spark plug ignites it, combustion takes place, and the force of the explosion drives the piston down—the power stroke.

As it slides down, the piston uncovers the exhaust port and at the same time compresses the new intake of fuel mixture in the crankcase, causing it to flow up into the combustion chamber and push out the exhaust gases. (*Figure 10*)

Everything has taken place during a single trip of the piston up and down.

Offhand it would seem as if this engine, by delivering twice as many power strokes, becomes twice as good as the four-stroke engine.

It has disadvantages, however, that keep it from being a good engine for cars. Its biggest drawback is that it will not run equally well at all speeds.

If we want to speed up an engine, we give it more gas. If we want to slow it down, we give it less gas. But when a two-stroke engine is given less gas, the amount of fresh mixture

Figure 11

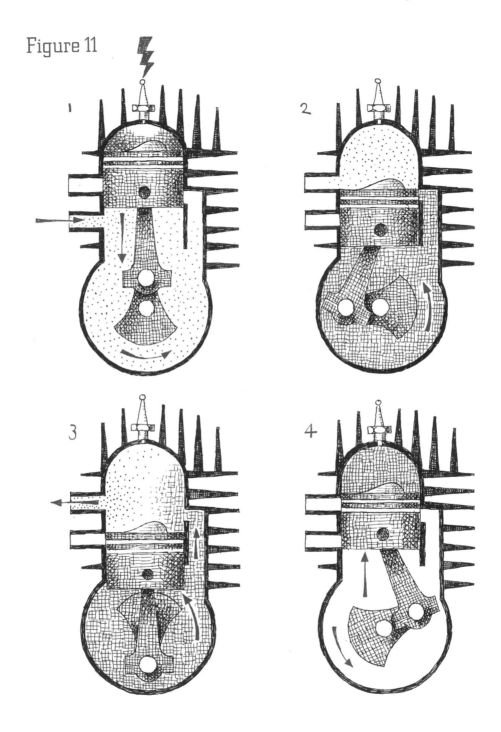

flowing into the cylinder may not be enough to push out the exhaust gases. Some of the exhaust gas stays in the combustion chamber, mixes with the fresh charge of fuel, and makes it burn less well. When you hear an engine cough or "miss," this is what has happened. The fuel is not burning properly.

The bump on the crown of the piston is there to help keep the fresh fuel and exhaust gases separated and prevent them from mixing. But if there is not enough fuel coming in, it cannot do its job thoroughly.

This is one of the main reasons the two-stroke engine is not used in cars. It works better on a smaller scale, however, and is used successfully for lawn mowers, outboard motors, lightweight motor bikes, pumps, and small generators.

For internal combustion engines to work well, the fuel must be burned up so completely during each explosion that nothing is left of it but exhaust gases which can be cleared completely from the cylinder.

If the fuel does not burn hotly and quickly enough, it will leave solid "ashes" in the form of carbon. This can do damage to the cylinder and piston by becoming mixed with the oil on their surfaces and grinding into them.

We have talked a lot about engines without stopping to find out how all these pieces of metal can rub against each other without wearing themselves out or getting too hot.

Modern engineering makes it possible to bore cylinders and turn out pistons so accurately that they fit together very closely.

In the days of the early steam engines, engineers were

lucky if a cylinder could be bored to fit a piston with no more than a quarter of an inch of daylight showing between them. It was a long time before this measurement was reduced to as little as a sixteenth of an inch. Considering this problem, it is easy to imagine how much steam leaked away around the edges of the piston and was lost before it could be used to produce work.

Today pistons fit inside cylinders to within a few thousandths of an inch. Their surfaces are highly polished, but they would soon grow very hot and scratch each other if they were not lubricated with oil. In fact this is true of *all* moving parts in a car, and some cars have as many as four hundred moving parts in the engine alone.

A film of oil must be kept constantly between the sides of the piston and the cylinder's walls. This alone will not keep them from becoming too hot, however, and if they become too hot the heat will crack them.

Some way must be found to keep them from overheating. In most cars this is done by surrounding the pistons with a jacket of water.

If you have ever looked at a car engine of the kind we are talking about, you know that it has a radiator in front of the engine.

This radiator is kept filled with water. The water is cooled by a fan, and, when the car is moving, by the air that rushes through the grille in the front of the hood.

When water flows through the jacket around the cylinders, it draws off some of their heat and thus keeps them cool enough to work efficiently.

Since this heat has been transferred to the water, the water becomes hot. But it is constantly flowing back and forth. It returns to the radiator and is cooled, then flows around to the cylinders again.

Besides the problems of lubrication and cooling, there is also the problem of sealing.

The fuel mixture and the force of its explosion must be kept sealed tightly inside the combustion chamber and not allowed to escape around the sides of the piston.

Rings are fitted around the piston to make it gas-tight. These press even more closely against the walls of the cylinder.

Before leaving the reciprocating piston engine, we should have a look at one more kind which works in a different and interesting way: the diesel engine.

You have probably noticed big trucks on the highways with a pipe running up their sides like a smokestack. Sometimes they let out a lot of black smoke that looks very bad, considering the air pollution that already exists.

As it happens, though, this smoke looks worse than it is. Diesel smoke does not put as much of the worst exhaust gases into the air as do the exhausts of ordinary cars that burn gasoline.

Instead of gasoline, diesel engines burn oil. Instead of mixing the oil with air in a carburetor, they spray the oil into air inside the combustion chamber. And instead of using a spark to set off the explosion, they use extremely high compression to make the fuel explode.

You will remember that the more a fuel mixture is compressed, the hotter it becomes. In a diesel engine cylinder the air is compressed until it becomes so hot the fuel catches fire.

Because they burn their fuel more efficiently, diesel two-stroke engines work much better than those that use gasoline, especially when they are supercharged.

A supercharger is a device with two rotors which revolve and force air into the cylinder. The fuel mixture does not enter the crankcase first, as it did in the two-stroke gasoline engine.

The piston forces the air in the chamber into a very small space. At this point an oil mist is sprayed into the densely compressed air, and the air is so hot that it makes the oil catch on fire and explode.

The piston is driven down, and an exhaust valve opens. The air rushing in from the supercharger pushes all the exhaust gases out before the next stroke begins. (*Figure 12*)

Although diesel fuel is cheaper than gasoline, and the diesel engine works very well, it has not been used very much as yet for passenger cars.

The reason is that diesel engines are more expensive to build. For one thing, since they use such high compression, they have to be more heavily built.

Imagine for a moment that you are blowing up a balloon.

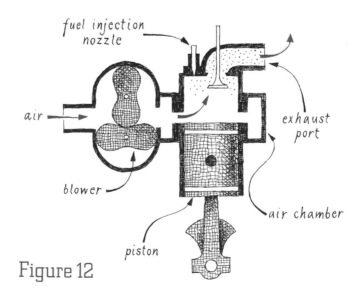

Figure 12

The balloon grows larger and larger. Finally it reaches a point where it cannot stretch any farther If you blow any more air into it now, it will break. You have filled it with higher compression than it can take.

Only if it were made of heavier, tougher rubber would it be able to withstand the extra compression caused by more air blown into the same limited space.

The same thing is true of cylinders in an engine. There is a limit to how much compression they can contain without breaking. That is why the diesel engine must be more heavily built.

Another difficulty is that their fuel injectors, the devices that spray oil into the combustion chamber, must be very precise and, therefore, are very expensive to make. The fuel injectors and the diesel's fuel pump cost much more than the gasoline engine's carburetor and electric system.

We have seen how piston engines work and what they can do. Now let's find out something about the Wankel rotary engine, starting with the man who invented it.

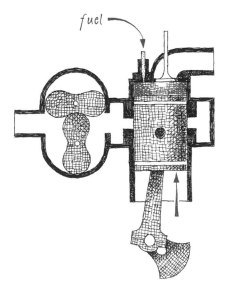

fuel

Figure 12

6

felix wankel

In 1902, when "horseless carriages" were just beginning to be taken seriously by many people, although few were on the roads as yet, a boy named named Felix Wankel was born in the Black Forest of Germany.

He might have stayed there all his life and never come closer to engineering than perhaps building a cuckoo clock were it not for World War I. His father was killed early in the war when Felix was only twelve. By the time the war was over, times were hard in Germany. Instead of continuing his education after high school, Felix Wankel moved to the city of Heidelberg to look for work in order to support himself and his widowed mother.

He found a job as salesman for a publisher of scientific books, but his heart was not in that sort of career. He spent his spare time tinkering with machinery and trying to think up ideas for making better machines—especially better engines.

At twenty-two he set up his own machine shop. At first he made his living by doing routine jobs, grinding cylinders, repairing motors. But in this way he learned important practical lessons, such as how to make machine parts that were accurately produced and worked well.

Before long he became interested in rotary engines. He continued his education by taking correspondence courses and attending night school, but always his mind was on rotary engines and how to make better ones.

This is not to say he disregarded other engines. In fact, the first patent he ever took out covered his design for a reciprocating piston engine. It involved a piston in a horizontal cylinder with a combustion chamber at each end and a crown on each end of the piston.

By that time, however, he was spending most of his working hours on the problem of seals, especially seals for rotary engines.

More than anything else, what was holding back the development of such engines was this problem of preventing the seeping away of gases, before and after combustion, from one part of the engine to another.

We will see later on how difficult this problem was in developing the Wankel engine.

By the time ten years had passed, Felix Wankel was no longer merely running a small machine shop. By then he had been hired by a large German car manufacturing firm to do research on rotary engines and new ideas for sealing. He did not get along with his new bosses, however, and soon switched firms to do the same sort of work for another car manufacturer.

But now he got into trouble, although the trouble had nothing directly to do with his work. It was at this time that Adolf Hitler and his Nazi political party were gaining power in Germany. Money was being stolen from a business firm by members of Hitler's party. Wankel helped bring the case to light.

Hitler was the kind of man who looked for revenge against everyone who ever opposed him in any way. He did not forget about Felix Wankel. When he came to power, he saw to it that Wankel was sent to jail as a "traitor."

Fortunately Wankel had friends who stood by him and worked for his release. After several months he was free again. And once he was out of prison he was quick to move his workshop from Heidelberg to his own native Black Forest village of Lahr.

A year later when Hermann Goering, head of the German air force, wanted him to come to Berlin to do his research and conduct his experiments, Wankel said he did not care to live in Berlin. Instead he talked Goering into building a research center for him even farther from Berlin, on a lake just across the border from Switzerland.

Whether Wankel was ever tempted to jump over into Switzerland during the years that followed is not known. Certainly he was no admirer of Hitler. But Germany was his native country, and he remained there.

He was given the task of building a rotary valve engine for the Luftwaffe, the German air force. He worked on this and other research assignments throughout World War II. His engine was built and tested, but the war ended before it could be produced for use in warplanes.

The war was hardly over before Wankel was in jail again.

Because he was an enemy engineer who had been working on airplane engines, the French called him a war criminal. Now he had gotten into trouble with both sides!

After keeping him in prison for a year the French released him, but saw to it that his research center was dismantled, and that he was not allowed to do any further research work for several years.

Finally the same good friend who had gotten him out of Hitler's jail was able to arrange for him to return to work. Wankel set up a new research center in 1951 on the shores of the same Lake Constance and very close to where his wartime shops had been located.

From that time forward he worked on the development of his new rotary engine, but it was still to be many years before the first car equipped with a Wankel engine would appear.

7

the wankel
rotary engine

The reciprocating piston engine and the rotary engine are both internal combustion engines, but their movements are quite different.

One engine has pistons. The other has rotors.

Pistons move up and down.

Rotors revolve.

To get the feeling of a piston's movement, hold your fist out at arm's length and move it quickly up and down with short, sharp strokes.

This is not easy to do. It takes a lot of energy to make your fist suddenly stop and go down, then stop and come up, and so on, again and again. Your whole body shakes from the effort.

Next, instead of moving your fist up and down, start swinging it in a circle—and always in the same direction, without having to stop and swing it around in the opposite direction.

Which is the easier motion? The circular one.

This is the principal reason why the rotary engine causes much less vibration than the piston engine.

And of course, if rotors can be made to revolve, they can make a shaft turn.

The piston's up-and-down motion can turn a shaft only if it is connected to a crank that can change its motion to a rotary motion. A rotary cranks a shaft to make it turn, too, but does so with its own rotary motion.

A rotor does the same work as a piston, but instead of moving up and down inside a cylinder it revolves inside a housing (the case that encloses it).

If it is going to make a shaft turn, however, the rotor cannot simply revolve on the shaft like a wheel on an axle. A rotor also needs the leverage which a cranking motion gives.

It is not hard to understand what leverage is, because it is something we all use in many different ways every day of our lives.

Many water faucets have straight handles which are good examples of a lever. If you take the handle off and try to turn on the water by twisting the shaft of the valve with your fingers, you will probably find it hard to turn. But turning the handle is easy, because the handle exerts the forces of leverage on the shaft.

When you want to loosen a nut on the end of a bolt, you use a pair of pliers or a wrench. Both of these are a form of lever, and in a sense you *crank* the nut off the bolt.

All that a wrench would need in order to become a crank would be to have its handle extended and bent at a right angle. But when we use a wrench, it is our arm that becomes the crank handle.

Suppose you tried to revolve a long, straight shaft by hand. You would find this was hard to do. But if you could fit a crank on the end of the shaft, you would be able to make it revolve much more easily.

The crank gives you *leverage*.

A rotor, then, must develop some sort of leverage if it is going to turn a shaft with the same sort of power a crank has. That is the main object of a car engine: to provide the power to make the shaft turn so that it can make the wheels turn.

What is a rotor, and how does it work?

A rotor is a moving part of an engine that revolves in a stationary part.

To make the rotor start revolving, it must be given a push with fuel.

In a cylinder, the fuel mixture exploding in the combustion chamber gives the piston the push that delivers the power stroke.

The rotor must also have a combustion chamber where the rotor can be given a push by exploding fuel. It must be enclosed in some sort of housing, so that the chamber can be created.

Let's start with a circular rotor, turning like a wheel.

Such a rotor can, of course, be enclosed in a circular housing.

But inside a circular housing there is no way to form a combustion chamber. A circle inside a circle does not close off any spaces between them. There is no way to close off a chamber in which the four steps—intake, compression, combustion, exhaust—can take place. *(Figure 13a)*

What we need are some straight sides that *will* divide the space into chambers. So let's change our circular rotor into a three-sided one. *(Figure 13b)*

Now we have three spaces closed off between the three tips of our triangular rotor.

But the trouble with this is that as the rotor swings around, the three chambers remain exactly the same size all the time.

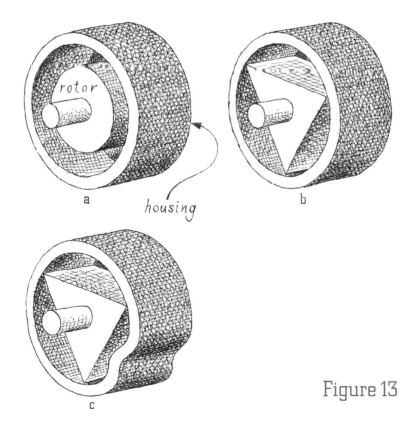

rotor

housing

a

b

c

Figure 13

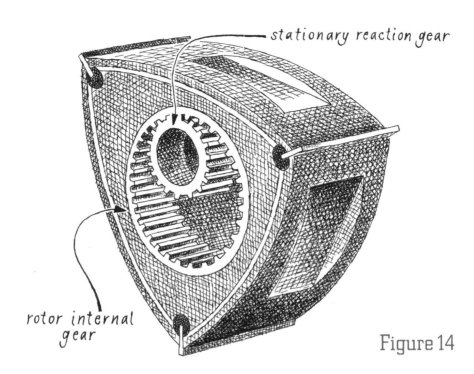

stationary reaction gear

rotor internal gear

Figure 14

If they do that, how can they compress a fuel mixture? It can't be done. If the rotor is going to compress its fuel mixture, its chambers must become smaller after they have been filled with fuel.

To make the chambers become smaller at some point along the path taken by the rotor as it swings around, we must bend in the edge of the housing.

Now we have a space which is smaller and will therefore compress the fuel mixture. *(Figure 13c)*

The only trouble with this is that now our rotor will no longer be able to revolve in the housing.

When they come to the bent-in part, the rotor tips will jam against it and our engine will be ruined.

What we need now is to find a way to make the tips slide past the bent-in part of the housing.

If the tips could only back away as they went past that part of the housing, everything would work fine.

How to do this has been known for a long time. Felix Wankel did not invent the method, but he made good use of it.

To make the rotor tips back away from the bent-in part of the housing, special gears must be used.

One gear is called the stationary reaction gear. It is fixed to the end cover plate of the housing. Its center is right on line with the shaft, but not connected to it. This gear does not revolve.

A larger gear is mounted in the center of the rotor, with its teeth pointing inward. These fit the teeth of the small gear.

The small gear does not move. The large gear rolls around it. And of course the rotor rolls around it, too, since the large gear is part of the rotor. (*Figure 14*)

This action is very much like that of a hula hoop. If you have ever put a hula hoop around your waist and managed to make it swing in a circle around you, you know that to keep it swinging you have to keep pressure constantly between your waist and the hoop. Your waist is always pressing against the hoop.

You are taking the part of the small gear. The hoop is taking the part of the large gear. The big difference is that in a rotor it is the large gear (the hoop) that is providing the power for the swing, while the small gear does not move.

As the rotor turns, then, its large gear "walks" around the small, stationary gear.

In this way part of the rotor is constantly drawing back from the path it would take if it were revolving on center, like a wheel. And of course the opposite side of the rotor is pushed out farther than it would be if the rotor were revolving on center.

The next question is, what sort of shape must the housing have now? How must it be shaped in order to fit with the strange path being taken by the rotor tips?

Felix Wankel solved this problem without the help of geometry, a subject he knew little about. Years later a mathematician showed him how it can be worked out on paper. We do not know exactly how Wankel went about finding the correct shape for his housing, but it is not hard to understand how it could be done.

Suppose we built a working model of the rotor and its gears and mounted the model on a table.

If we attached a pencil to one of the rotor tips, with its point touching the table top, and then revolved the rotor, the pencil would trace the path followed by the rotor tip. It would draw the pattern for the housing.

It is interesting, however, to see how this can be worked out on paper.

To begin with, we use two circles.

The distance from the center of a circle to its edge, or circumference, is called its radius.

The large circle can have a radius that is twice as long as

Figure 15

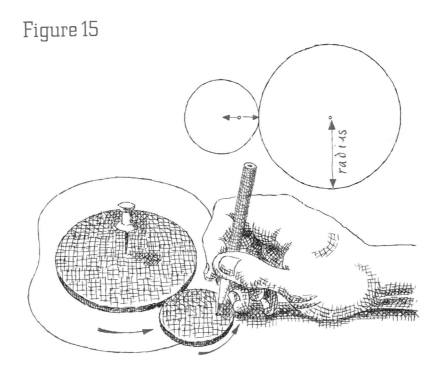

the small circle, or three times as long—it does not matter, just so long as the ratio of the two radii is an even amount. In other words, one cannot be one and a half times as long as the other.

Our large circle has a radius that is twice as long as our small circle's radius.

Now, imagine that we roll the small circle, without slipping, around the circumference of the large circle.

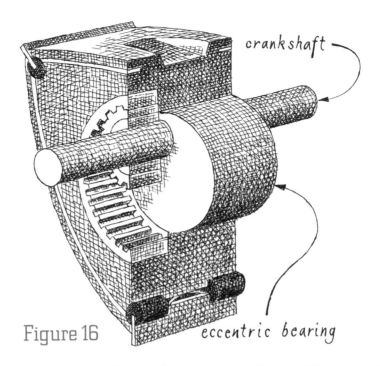

crankshaft

eccentric bearing

Figure 16

Suppose we put a dot in the center of the small circle. What path will that dot follow?

Since it will always be the same distance from the center of the large circle, the dot will trace a circular path and make a perfect circle around the large circle.

Suppose we put the dot on the circumference of the small circle. What path will it now follow?

Now its path will look quite different. Starting from the circumference of the large circle, it will roll out and then in again, halfway around.

But, now let's put the dot off center in the small circle, halfway between its center and its circumference. What path will it now follow?

This time, when the small circle has rolled all the way around the large circle, the dot will trace a shape that looks like a fat figure-eight.

This is the shape our triangular rotor's housing must have. In geometry, it is called an epitrochoid. *(Figure 15)*

Since the large gear is swinging the rotor around with a hula-hoop motion, the rotor has to be connected to the shaft by a special bearing. It is called an eccentric bearing, because it is off-center.

This bearing is like a lever. It makes it possible for the rotor to *crank* the shaft and make it revolve. *(Figure 16)*

Now we will see how the rotor tips travel around inside the epitrochoidal housing, each tip always touching the sides without jamming against them at any point. We will see how chambers are formed, so that intake, compression, combustion, and exhaust can take place inside the housing.

Now we will see how the Wankel rotary engine actually works.

8

the wankel engine
in action

The Wankel rotor is not a flat-sided triangle. Its sides are bulged out slightly. These curved surfaces make the rotor faces fit more closely against the face of the housing in certain positions. The face of each side has a broad groove in it. This makes it work better as a compression chamber. *(Figure 17)*

The Wankel engine goes through the same cycle as the reciprocating piston engine, but there is a big difference in the way the power is produced.

In the piston engine the four phases of the cycle take place one at a time in the combustion chamber.

In the Wankel, three of the four phases are always taking place at the same time—but in different working chambers.

The three tips of the rotor divide the Wankel into three

working chambers, in each of which the four phases take place in succession.

To begin with let's follow one chamber through the entire cycle. We can do this by looking at the sketches in Figure 18.

In these sketches the rotor is turning clockwise (in the same direction a clock's hands move). In the course of the twelve sketches it makes one complete revolution and completes the four-part cycle:

1. The Wankel does not have pistons. Instead, like the two-stroke gasoline and diesel engines, it has an intake port and an exhaust port. Here side A of the rotor is covering both ports. As it has swung around to this position it has swept the last of the exhaust gases left by the previous cycle out through the exhaust port.

At the instant shown here, it covers the intake port closely enough to cut off most of the intake of fuel mixture, though not all, because the surface of A is not tight against the port. The rotor faces never quite touch the face of the housing. Only the three tips slide against it. It is the tips that seal off one chamber from the others.

2. Now A is swinging away from the intake port, allowing fuel mixture to flow in.

Notice in this and the next two sketches how A's working chamber grows larger and larger. This means that the same sort of thing is happening to this chamber as happened to the piston engine's chamber when the piston slid down after emptying the cylinder of exhaust gases. A partial vacuum is formed, and the fuel mixture is sucked into it.

THE WANKEL ENGINE IN ACTION

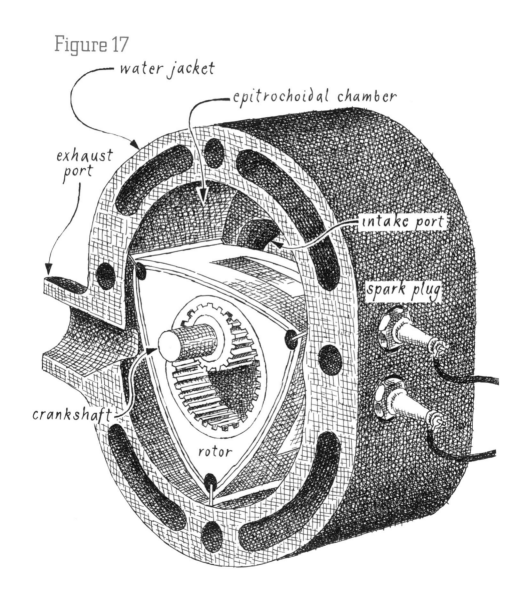

Figure 17

water jacket

epitrochoidal chamber

exhaust
port

intake port

spark plug

crankshaft

rotor

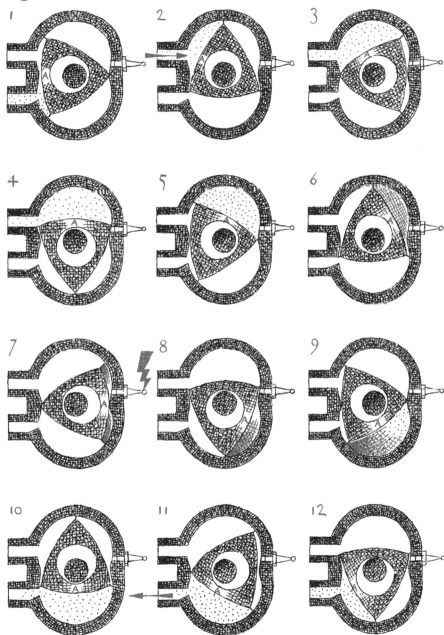

Figure 18

3. The chamber is growing larger.

4. Now A is straight across the narrow part of the fat figure-eight, and the chamber has reached its largest volume. In another instant A's trailing tip will cross the intake port and will stop the flow of fuel into the chamber.

5. Now the chamber is becoming smaller again. The fuel mixture is being compressed into a smaller and smaller space.

6. The chamber continues to shrink in size. By the time A swings against the figure-eight "waist" in the next sketch, the fuel mixture will be compressed into a very small space.

   Notice where the spark plug is placed, ready to produce the spark that will make the fuel explode.

7. BOOM! Combustion takes place.

8. The force of the explosion is pushing against A, which is now swinging toward the lower end of the figure-eight. This is the power stroke that keeps A moving.

9. The explosion continues and finishes, burning up the fuel mixture and leaving only exhaust gases in the chamber.

10. Now A's leading tip has crossed the exhaust port and uncovered it, so that the exhaust gases can escape.

11. Side A begins to push out the exhaust gases.

12. The chamber grows smaller and smaller again, forcing the exhaust gases out faster. And now, if we look back at the first sketch, we can see how the last of the exhaust gases are being swept out and the whole cycle is about to begin again.

In the course of this one revolution, A delivered one power stroke (see sketches 7, 8, and 9). But in the meantime the other two faces of the rotor have also made one revolution and have each delivered a power stroke, too.

In one revolution the rotor has delivered *three* power strokes.

At all times one of the four parts of the cycle is taking place in each of the three chambers, and always, of course, a different one in each chamber. The position of the chamber at any instant during a revolution determines what is taking place inside it.

Let's look now at the set of sketches in Figure 19 showing all three chambers in action at once:

1. While A is sweeping out the last of its exhaust gases and is about to begin intake, B is compressing its fuel mixture and C is receiving a power stroke from the exploding mixture expanding in its chamber.

2. Now A is taking in fuel, B is close to finishing compression, and C is ready to push out its exhaust gases.

3. A has almost finished taking in fuel, B's explosion is being set off by the spark, and C is pushing out exhaust gases.

4. A is full of fuel mixture and about to close off the intake port, B is receiving its power stroke from the expanding gases of its explosion, and C is about to get rid of the last of its exhaust gases.

Notice that in the course of these four sketches, the rotor has only made one-third of a revolution. Each chamber has gone through only one-third of its four-part cycle.

THE WANKEL ENGINE IN ACTION

Figure 19

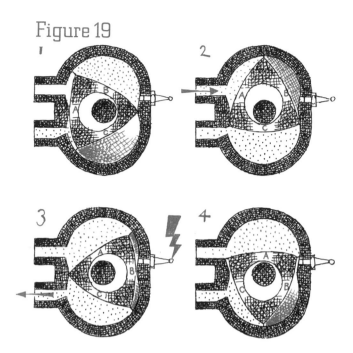

Describing the workings of the Wankel rotary engine in this way makes the whole operation sound easy. Many special problems had to be solved, however, before the engine could operate successfully.

For example, each of the "phasing gears," as the two gears are called, has a certain number of teeth. The number of teeth in the phasing gears had to be decided. Just any number will not do.

It was found that the ratio between the gears must be three to two. For every two teeth the small stationary gear has, the large gear must have three.

If the small gear has twenty-four teeth, the large gear must have thirty-six. If the small gear has thirty-six teeth, the large gear must have fifty-four.

Given this ratio, every time the rotor makes a full revolution its gear-wheel has walked around the small gear exactly one and one half times. In two revolutions it goes around the small gear three times. Every other revolution brings the two gears back into the same position and keeps the rotor swinging in exactly the same way each time it turns.

The hardest problem of all was sealing.

Everything depends on the three tips of the rotor, which must shut off each chamber tightly from the others.

Let's look once more at the third sketch in Figure 19.

Suppose the three rotor tips did not seal off the three working chambers from one another.

Then fuel mixture from A would seep into B, where combustion is already taking place, and combustion would spread back into A. Exhaust gases from C would seep into A, fouling the fresh fuel mixture coming in through the intake port. It would also seep into B and spoil combustion there. The engine would work poorly, or not at all.

How could strips of metal be fitted into the rotor tips in such a way as to press against the face of the housing so firmly at all times that no gases could get past them in either direction?

For one thing, there had to be springs under the strips to keep them pressed firmly against the housing. And of course there had to be lubrication between the two metal surfaces—the rotor tips and the face of the housing. A film of oil had to be kept between them so that they would not scratch each other and so that the tips would slide smoothly.

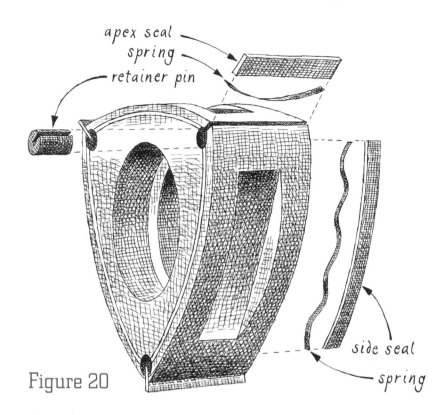

apex seal
spring
retainer pin
side seal
spring

Figure 20

These tips are also called apexes, and the strips of metal fitted into them are called apex seals. (*Figure 20*)

One of the difficulties in making these apex seals press tightly against the face of the housing at all times and in all positions was the problem of the leaning angle.

If you will look closely at the sketches of the rotor in action, you will see that the tips are almost never pressing straight up and down against the housing. Only at the narrowest point of the figure-eight's waist are they straight up and down.

The rest of the time they are leaning against it at sharper angles.

The sharper this angle becomes, the harder it is for the seals to press against the face of the housing. If the angle becomes more than 30°, there is likely to be trouble.

This is one reason why the triangular rotor has proved to be the best design—for it is possible to build rotors with four sides, and even five. But in each instance the housing must have one more side, too: if the rotor has four sides, the housing must have three; if the rotor has five sides, the housing must have four, as shown in Figure 21.

In four-sided rotors, the leaning angle becomes as much as 41.8°, and in the five-sided rotor it reaches as much as 56.4°. In both cases, compression drops to levels too low for good combustion.

The three-sided rotor in the fat figure-eight works best, because the leaning angle of its apex seals is never more than 30°.

Figure 21

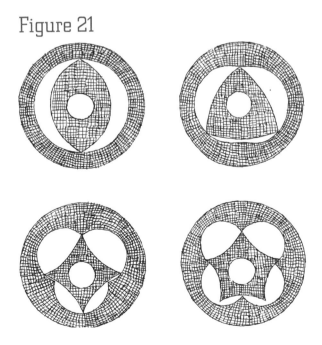

For an interesting reason, combustion also posed some special problems.

In a piston engine the fuel mixture enters a chamber in which, once it is inside, it does not move around. But in a Wankel rotary engine the fuel mixture enters a chamber that is moving fast in a circular direction. While it is being compressed, the fuel is being swept forward very rapidly.

When the spark ignites it, the fuel is traveling fast, and part of it is ahead of the spark. The flame has to catch up with it and burn it all at once or the explosion will not be a good one.

The flame front, as it sweeps forward burning the fuel mixture, has a hard time keeping up with the "gas transfer velocity" (a new term that is not needed for piston engines, where combustion is stationary).

In some Wankel engines, two spark plugs are used for each rotor, so that all the fuel mixture can be ignited at once. In others, ways have been found to make one spark plug do the job well enough for the engine to run satisfactorily.

But this problem, along with the others, is still being worked on by the engineers who are developing the Wankel engine and trying to make it perform ever more efficiently.

Now that we have learned something about how the Wankel rotary engine works, the next question is, what advantages does it offer? Can it really replace the reciprocating piston engine in the motorcar world?

9

advantages
of the
wankel engine

On the first page of this book it was pointed out that other engines have been used in cars, but in the past none has been able to challenge the piston engine. To do so, a new engine would have to be at least some of the following things:

Cheaper to build.
Cheaper to run.
Smaller and lighter with the same power.
More dependable and long-lasting.
Easier to repair.
Quieter and more nearly vibration-free.

It is time now to put the Wankel rotary engine up against this list of requirements and see how it makes out.

Cheaper to build? Yes. When Wankel engines are produced on a large scale, they may cost only half as much as a piston engine of similar horsepower.

One manufacturer made a direct comparison between a Wankel engine rated at 185-horsepower and an American V8 engine rated at 195-horsepower.

The V8 (an eight-cylinder engine) cost about $2 per horsepower to build. The Wankel, if similarly mass-produced, would cost about $1 per horsepower. Even now Wankel engines are being produced for about 25 percent less than a comparable piston engine would cost.

The V8 has a total of 1,029 parts, the Wankel only 633.

In the V8 there are 388 *moving* parts, in the Wankel only 154—less than half as many.

Cheaper to run? Here is the only requirement the Wankel has not yet managed to measure up to.

About 18 to 19 miles per gallon is the best mileage it has produced so far. Many compact cars with piston engines give 25 to 30 miles per gallon. Now that the energy crisis has made gasoline so expensive, this becomes an important consideration. Yet a good deal of the difference may be recovered in other ways, through savings on repairs and maintenance, and extra years of dependable service.

For that matter, even in the area of fuel the Wankel engine offers some advantages. It works well on cheaper, low octane gasoline. It gives good mileage at cruising speeds on city streets where many cars, especially large ones, get as little as 5 or 6 miles per gallon.

The Wankel needs to have a quart of oil added about every

1,000 miles, but it never has to have its oil changed, because its oil does not get dirty. The new oil can simply be added to the old, and this of course saves money—especially at today's prices for oil.

Smaller and lighter with the same power? Yes, very definitely. The Wankel, at 237 pounds, weighed less than half as much as the V8 at 607 pounds, and took up only a quarter as much space.

If an engine can be made smaller and lighter with the same power, then cars can be designed better. With a lower, smaller hood in front of him, the driver will have better vision.

And if the engine takes up less space, that leaves more space to be used inside the car, making the driver and his passengers more comfortable.

A lighter engine also means that the whole car will weigh less, and less weight causes less wear on the brakes and tires.

Wankel engines usually have two rotors. If more power is needed, however, more rotors can be added to the same engine. Three or four rotors would produce a great increase in power over two—but also an increase in size. Most motorcar companies working with the Wankel engine are using twin-rotor engines.

In this book we have been concentrating on engines for motorcars, but it is interesting to note here another of the Wankel engine's general advantages: it is not limited by any "scale effect," which means that it can be built to almost any scale or size and still work well.

This is not true of all motors. Many motors work well if built on a large scale, but not if built on a small scale, or vice versa. But Wankel engines of 3-horsepower and 1,000-horse-power have both been built, and work equally well. Wankel engines can power everything from lawn mowers and outboard motors to big electric generators.

More dependable and long-lasting? A Japanese car with a Wankel engine was given a hard test by being driven 30,000 miles by various drivers over a period of eighteen months, in all sorts of driving conditions and on all sorts of roads.

The gas mileage settled down to an average of 18.5 miles per gallon. A quart of oil was added every 1,000 miles, but the oil was never changed.

When the car had gone 30,000 miles the engine was taken out and carefully examined.

Since the apex seals get the most wear, they were of special interest. Had they held up all right, or were they worn out?

On the road the rotor was usually turning at about 2,000 revolutions per minute—over thirty times every second. And every second of that time the apex seals were sliding around the face of the housing like racers on a track, at an average speed of 103 feet per second. That speed would win a 100-yard dash in less than three seconds. It is over 70 miles per hour.

But the apex seals always slide in the same direction, while the piston rubs the cylinder walls in both directions.

A new apex seal is 10 millimeters high (one centimeter, less than half an inch). Measurements of the apex seals after 30,000 miles ranged between 9.98 and 9.49 mm (millimeters).

They are supposed to be replaced when they have worn down to 8 mms, but will actually continue to work efficiently until they have worn down to between 6 and 7 mm.

So there was plenty of wear left in them, as much as 60,000 to 70,000 more miles' worth, allowing for the increased rate of wear they would suffer as the face of the housing also began to wear (although after 30,000 miles its wear was still too small to measure). At that rate the seals would be good for at least a total of 100,000 miles, and perhaps more.

The phasing gears were like new.

Since the rotors are spinning around in the housing, they also have to have side seals—rings to keep gases from seeping down the sides of the rotor. (See Figure 20, p. 56.) These get much less hard wear than the apex seals, and showed very little wear when examined.

All in all, it looked as if the Wankel engine could be counted on to last a long time.

Easier to repair? With only about half as many parts, and less than half as many working parts, the Wankel is much easier to repair.

Again, it is the apex seals that are most likely to need replacement, and a technique is being developed which will make this job easy.

It is something like the push-pull working of an injector safety razor, where a new blade is slid in as the old one is slid out. This can be done without even taking the engine apart, and once it is done the engine is as good as new.

Quieter and more nearly vibration-free? Because the rotor is revolving instead of pounding up and down like a piston, the Wankel makes a humming sound rather than a clatter. And its revolving motion can be balanced so well that the car is almost completely free of vibration. This, of course, makes riding more comfortable.

One other point should be considered, and that is the question of air pollution.

The exhaust gases from an engine travel through the car's muffler and tail pipe out into the air. They are one of the most serious causes of air pollution.

Three kinds of gases are given off by car exhausts: hydrocarbons (HC), carbon monoxide (CO), and oxides of nitrogen (NOx).

Emission control equipment (devices which can be attached to cars to reduce the amount of gases that escape to pollute the air) are being developed, but it is found that of the three gases involved, NOx is the hardest to control.

The Wankel engine puts out about the same amount of HC and CO as a comparable piston engine—but only about a third as much NOx. This is a definite advantage as far as air pollution control is concerned. In fact, the question of air pollution, and of protecting our environment in general, may have more to do with the future of the Wankel rotary engine than anything else.

It looks as if, after a few more years of development and improvement, the Wankel engine may have a good chance of replacing the reciprocating piston engine in our cars. But will our need for clean air, and our growing shortage of such fuels as oil and gasoline, force us to develop a completely new kind of engine for our cars, our boats, our ships, our trains, and our electric generators?

What are some of the other possibilities? Let's have a look at some of them.

10

engines
of the
future

Better engines have become a vital necessity because of the energy crisis and our need to reduce air pollution. Every possibility is being explored, and many new engines are being developed and tried out.

Of course, great efforts are being made to improve the reciprocating piston engine itself, through such means as electronic fuel injection and stratified charge.

Electronic fuel injection eliminates the carburetor and greatly reduces the cost of the engine. A simple computerlike control checks up on such factors as combustion temperature and pressure, engine speed, and air flow. Each piston then receives the exact amount of fuel it needs for each of its strokes. This increases efficiency and reduces waste.

Stratified charge varies the fuel-to-air ratio in combustion chambers so that more gas is concentrated near the spark plug, where it will burn faster and more completely. This means that less gas escapes without being burned up, or being only partly burned, and thus there is less pollution of the air from the exhaust fumes.

But the piston engine still depends on gasoline as its fuel, and this may mean that its days are numbered, no matter how much it is improved. This may also be true of the Wankel engine—but the day when other fuels can replace gasoline is still many years away. It is not likely that engines using other fuels will be able to challenge the gasoline engine before 1980 at the earliest.

Another gasoline engine that many believe may take over the field is the turbine engine, especially the Williams Turbine Clean-Air Engine.

Turbines are rotary engines that fan air into a combustion chamber where it mixes with fuel. In this engine, fuel is burned continuously instead of a bit at a time. This continuous burning reduces air pollution from exhaust gases. The Williams engine has two turbines, one behind the other, and the second turbine is driven by the exhaust gases of the first. The engine's high combustion temperatures, however, produce a great amount of oxides of nitrogen (NOx). And, once again, it is still a gasoline engine.

What about engines that do not have to depend on gasoline?

One of these is the Stirling "hot air" engine.

In this engine pistons move up and down in chambers—but

these are not combustion chambers. The Stirling engine is an *external* combustion engine. The chambers are filled with hydrogen gas which is alternately heated and cooled to push the piston up and down. The top of the chamber is heated from an outside source.

To provide this heat, the Stirling engine can use almost any fuel—which means any new fuel that may be developed which causes less pollution than gasoline, or perhaps no pollution at all.

A second contender among new engines is, surprisingly enough, our old friend the steam engine! New metals and modern engineering have produced the Hinckley rotary steam engine, which offers light weight, moderate cost, and reduced air pollution. But with the Hinckley steam engine, as with the Stirling engine, it is much too soon to say whether either can be developed to the point of actually providing an engine that will meet the needs of our motorcars.

One of the greatest hopes for the future is the electric car, which would run silently and cause almost no air pollution. A car run by electricity would have very few moving parts and would be easy to maintain and repair. But at the present time, in order to furnish an electric car with enough power, it would have to carry so large and heavy a battery that it would be impractical.

What is needed is a fuel-cell battery whose energy-to-weight ratio is much higher than that of today's standard lead-acid batteries, the kind that are used in our present motorcars. Not until a revolutionary new battery replaces the ones we now have is the electric car likely to become the answer to our needs.

ENGINES OF THE FUTURE

Only one thing seems certain, and that is that the motorcar engine of the future will be quite different from the engines of today. In the meantime, however, it may well be the Wankel engine that will bridge the gap—and who can be sure some new fuel may not be powering it many years from now?

glossary

BATTERY: an automobile battery is a black box in which electricity is produced and stored.

BOILER: a metal tank in which water is heated and converted into steam.

CAM: a wheel with a projection on one side; a lopsided wheel.

CARBURETOR: a device which mixes air and a spray of gasoline into explosive fuel.

COMBUSTION: the catching fire and burning of fuel.

COMBUSTION CHAMBER: the space in a cylinder where fuel is compressed, ignited, and burned.

COMPRESSION: the squeezing together of fuel into a smaller space.

CRANKSHAFT: a shaft which drives or is driven by a series of cranks.

CYLINDER: a tube inside which a piston slides up and down.

ECCENTRIC BEARING: a metal cylinder, usually solid in this case, mounted off-center on a shaft.

ENERGY: the ability to do work.

ENGINE: a machine that can turn energy into mechanical force and action.

EXHAUST: the escape of waste or burned gases from an engine.

FLAME FRONT: the forward edge of a charge of burning fuel.

GEAR: a wheel with pins or teeth on its rim or along its sides.

HORSEPOWER: a unit of power based on the amount of work a horse would do in lifting 150 pounds to a height of 220 feet, an amount which is called 33,000 foot-pounds.

INTAKE: the taking in of fuel.

LEVER: a device, such as a crowbar or a tire iron, used to exert pressure or sustain weight.

PISTON: a round plug that is made to slide up and down inside a cylinder.

PORT: a round hole in a cylinder used for fuel intake or the escape of exhaust gases.

RADIATOR: a device used for cooling the water that circulates around an engine housing.

ROTOR: a rotating wheel in an engine.

SHAFT: in an engine, a shaft is a cylindrical metal bar.

SPARK PLUG: a device which produces electrical sparks to catch fuel on fire.

SUPERCHARGER: a device with two rotors which revolve and force air into the cylinder's combustion chamber.

VALVE: a form of stopper that can open to let air or steam or gas into a cylinder, and close to keep it out.

index